DRUNKEN THOUGHTS

ARIJIT MAJUMDAR

Made with ♥ on the Notion Press Platform
www.notionpress.com

Contents

Contents

Seeing an abyss out front

We Jump into a Life of shackle,

Wait till the bottom clears

Even the Devil was once an Angel...

Publisher Details

Rhythmic Publishers

-Seeking harmony through words.

We, at *Rhythmic Publications*, believe in the power of words as a means of seeking harmony in a chaotic universe. We are eager to provide aspiring writers with a premium platform to express themselves. Attractive packages are available for both solo books and anthologies (editorial services and book design included). We work diligently to make a book the best version of itself and client satisfaction is our top priority.

Contact us on:

Instagram: @rhythmicpublishers

E-mail: rhythmicpublications23@gmail.com

We are also on **Twitter** and **LinkedIn**

About The Author

Arijit Majumdar is a poet, scriptwriter, content editor and part time musings collector. He has been writing since last 5 years. He has written for many social media pages. His write up, "A Letter to December's Calcutta", is a renowned piece and has been printed in different magazines throughout India. He has also put some great inputs in the field of scriptwriting. He has written 2 voiceover series of his own.

Born and brought up in Kolkata, Arijit grabs his content searching his city and bits from his life and from the people around. He generally writes about the daily happenings of anybody's life which people can easily relate to. But mostly he considers himself to be a Poet. For him, movies and series that get you thinking and calm your soul are the perfect definition of taking a break. Satyajit Ray, Bob Dylan and Rupam Islam have inspired him on his journey of becoming a writer.

Arijit has also won much recognition in the field of writing. Besides his writing career, he is a B.Tech. Graduate working in an IT Firm. His daily routine doesn't allow him to squeeze writing sessions in between his working hours. However, he manages to mitigate all the walls to at least pen down some of his works on a page.

Follow the author on Instagram: @nonchalant_writer

About The Book

"Drunken Thoughts' is a collection of poems and musings. Some of it is inspired from real events and lessons and few are completely fictional but solely based on everyday life. Some might feel the book is too straightforward, but if somebody dives down into the pages, their idea might change. Life is a natural process and that's what this book tries to pinpoint. The irregularity of the writings was purposefully put in because, like our daily life, the book also doesn't have to be in sync. It can go higher or lower as our thoughts. The purpose of this book is to uplift the so-called bad phases of Life and to show that few words that you bleed through ink can heal you up. The book portrays that life is like an uneven road which you have to cross. Eventually one finds the way to move on and to forgive everything. A few poems are blunt and heart-wrenching but that's the beauty of it. The writings are the best collection from the pages of the author's diary. It also gives deep insight into a troubled yet happy soul for whom Life has a fixed definition. Losing hope is a stinging indictment to society and this book challenges that.

Prologue

I wondered the same. Why will a book full of poems and musings have a prologue? Maybe it was necessary or is just here to eclipse the fact that this book doesn't have a construct meaning. It is nothing but a thought journal of a whimsical introvert minded guy who prefers to sit in the corner of a room.

Do I suggest you to validate your inner self after numbing your senses? Absolutely not. That rush of memories and regrets are worse than a splinter. It wrecks your heart and shatters your soul into pieces. But sometimes the only option that remains within your grasp is facing the harsh reality. As Kafka says, "I have the true feeling of myself only when I am unbearably unhappy." Unless your pillow is wet at 3:00 in the morning, you do not get the true sense of the bitterness your soul holds. Why do we always point fingers to a particular fact and conclude, that was the sole reason for the state that we are in? Is it so easy to label and define the ideal reason of your self-loathing? Feeling is a compilation of all the situations and memories that your life holds. It is better to analyse every second that made you question yourself.

First, I thought of arranging the writings of this book in a chronological manner. It would have started with a good and cheerful note but would have ended in the most grating way. But an idea struck my mind. Why not write it the way feelings and mind simultaneously worked? Highs and lows are not predefined in here. Just like our usual life.

The words and feelings that I chose to portray here are not just restricted to me. These words are somewhat similar to any stranded soul on those busy streets. Sometimes you have to vent out. Your soul doesn't let you. It keeps those agonies and tears buried deep down teaching you a lesson throughout the rest of your journey.

You might find some of it to be obnoxious but you must understand the reason of the sombre note.

A sense of sonder is not a piece of cake but a process.

Journeys are beautiful,
Cherish each moment to the fullest.

1. A Letter to December's Calcutta

To December's Calcutta,

A Month where the city takes the last few Breaths of the Year. A Month of Well Wishes. A Month of Friendship. A Month of Celebration. A Month filled with Makes and Breaks.

When the city snoozes under a cloak of fog and regrets, the Neon lights of this City guide your remaining path. Where love breaks and builds in every corner of this City. A glass of Rum keeps you warm enough from those chilly uncalled winds.

A Month where your pasts haunt you. A month where puffs of smoke intertwine with thick layers of magic white dust in the air. The bright lights are just a few days aid to those Damaged Souls. Christmas carols and that crazy crowd of Park Street reminds everyone that the 365-day-countdown is finally coming to an end. A pleasant Sunday Afternoon with a bit of sunlight peeping through the clouds and those jumpers contrast perfectly. After 11 months of Struggles, Fights, Tears, Breakdowns, it narrows down to one thing: This Year is finally at its END. A New Year and a New Beginning. But like that December, the eagerness to be on track with those goals suddenly gets derailed.

Suddenly, those promises of New Years Eve with "The One" get lost. Another December approaches. Slowly and steadily, you get used to it. But some things do stay: Those sudden plans. Chilly Winter Night Outings and "Fake Sleepovers." Some people leave the city in search of New Destinations. Some stay back, because Calcutta in December is a mysterious land holding some deep secrets within itself.

When slowly and steadily the month passes away, you wait for it again with the same Old City and with a little bit of expectation and sometimes with someone who means "Something More Than Anything."

December's Calcutta teaches you to "Survive Alone and Fight" and it also teaches to "Keep your Loved Ones closer and hold them tight."

2. Grow

Look outside of your window
It's the winter hue,
Take that blanket off
Let that metamorphosis grow.
Seek for your long-lost love
Tightly embrace your hands,
Around their arms.
Let the silence soak in,
Close the gaps in between.
It's December
The end and the beginning settle down into one,
Fill the void you have in deep
Have your long-lasting epiphany.
Another book awaits
The pages are empty,
The chapters are your sole duty
But remember…
Last judge is your destiny.

3. Soul

You stood on the ledge
When everything started falling,
You called for help
But nothing kept you going.
Every night of yours
Was a Nightmare to your Efficacy,
You asked for a Voice
You got a Soul showering Peace.
Your Call for Help
Was like a Siren wailing,
You wanted a hand to grab
You got a backbone standing.
Slowly you mended
The tears got dried,
You got your track
But something already faded.
You never looked back
You never asked again,
Should have looked just for once
The Soul was never seen again…

4. A Close One Is All You Need

Agonies getting darker
Cutting down your strings,
Love can make you better
One that always rings.
Steadiness is falling apart
Entering the gloomy days,
Oppressed by the Society
Need for someone who stays.
Envy is not an option
Isolating is not a tradition
Sense of relief is your ambition
Attention is not the only solution.
Leaving your problems behind
Longing for the long-lost days,
Yearning for the one in mind
Open up to the one who stays.
Ugliness is a part of life
Needs are down to one
Easing up your way of life.
Eagerness guides your different ways,

Dire need of someone who stays….
First letters of each line make up
A CLOSE ONE IS ALL YOU NEED

5. Solitude

Bent down by Problems?
Searching for the shore,
Failed in your Dreams
Life felt no more.
Sitting on the shore
Watching the waves,
Loneliness getting heavier
Time gently sways.
Fighting for your survival
Gives a fragment of hope,
Fight or watch your burial
Void of escaping Scope.
Watch the sun setting down
Last Ray slowly fading,
It's time to get back to the town
The cycle is never ending.

6. Fate

Standing on the top
Thinking about the future,
Hold on to that thought
Fate leaves the last mark.
Fate is a small word
Yet plays a fatal part,
Getting on board?
Wait, until it falls apart.
Expecting a miracle
Everything's going to be alright,
But it ended in a debacle
Even if you fought right.
Nothing's going to be easy
Get that in mind,
All paths are little messy
Fate is one of a kind.

7. Imperishable Memories

I don't remember the Day we met,
But I do remember the Day you walked away.
I don't remember the Friendship goals,
But I do remember the mockery of my character.
I don't remember the Unbreakable Promises,
But I do remember the Brutus play.
I don't remember the Cigarettes and Beer,
But I do remember the Last Cup of Tea.
I don't remember the Long Walks,
But I do remember the Last Sight of your Eyes.
I don't remember the Hypocritical Note,
But I do remember the Last Call.
I don't remember the Pseudo Freud Speech.
But I do remember the Point of View.
I don't remember the False Hopes of Togetherness.
But I do remember the Day I waited.

8. To all those Stranded Souls

Yes, you loved somebody. You gave your everything in return of nothing. You waited. You helped. You stitched. But at the end, you were torn up mending someone else.

You try to give everything that you were left out from. You think giving them will help you get those Cloud 9 feelings beneath your feet. But that's just a few days aid. What happens when that band aid rips off? That scar remains. Maybe a bigger scar takes its place but it remains.

You search for the time you need irrespective of your feelings and worth. That small pocket watch gets thrashed by those who kill your every second. But remember, time heals. A bucket of hot water cools down eventually, even if it's in a hot weather. All it takes is patience and those valuable ticking seconds.

When you sit alone, and that clock in your room hits you with that tick, listen to it. With every tick, time passes by and so do the wounds. You loved somebody. You gave your everything and you got nothing. Does that mean you're at fault? No...And that doesn't stop you from locking those feelings. Cherish and embrace those. Those Feelings are your Soul Right....

9. Truth

Stranded with Thoughts
Whom to tell?
Nothing to utter
Hush! Everybody Stay!
Waits up a Long-Lost Road
Ahead of a Tired Soul,
Thinking of taking the First Step?
Regrets rush in at the Last Step.
Questioning its Presence
Every glass is a lullaby,
Every smoke it takes
Burns out that grim lie.
Taking its sole steps
Life suddenly stands at the back,
Ask for its final verdict
Before... The Last Stab.

10. A Closure you don't want to have…

I remember their name.
But I don't remember them as persons.
I remember the deeds they did.
But I don't remember the way we met.
I remember the countless backstabs
But I don't remember the conversations over Coffee.
I remember the ghosting.
But I don't remember the endless conversations.
I remember the feelings and depths.
But I don't remember the words you said.
I remember the countless lies.
But I don't remember the truth of trust.
You want that closure?
But I think you aren't "READY" yet.

11. Maybe...

I Still remember the Day I met You,
It was a pleasant morning in the Hue.
When everything was Falling apart,
You Sprung out of the Mist.
With loads of Craziness and Calmness,
You sustained that Mischievous Peace.
Chords were played correctly,
Otherwise, it would have been different lyrics.
Slowly the Chapters Turned,
The story unveiled with a Different Stand.
As your Smile was revealed,
My view towards the World came to a halt.
Your Eyes spoke a Different Language,
Unveiling some Deep Emotions within itself.
Your Path isn't easy,
But who said you have to search for a stick?
Your Wolf Power,
Surely portrays a Different Lone Strength.
Even if you fall,
A Pair of Hands will always help you to crawl
If the words get short with Time,
Replace it with those Old Chimes.

As the Sun Sets and the Moon shines
I wish to stay between the Eternity of Day and Night with YOU…

12. Reality

I see those Empty streets,
I see Loneliness.
I see those tall trees,
I see Confidence.
I see those Stray dogs,
I see Survivors.
I see those Shelter less,
I see Fighters.
I see those lost lovers,
I see Tiredness.
I see those Lost Stories,
I see Bitterness.
I see those Vagabonds,
I see Escapists.
I see those Escape Stories,
I see Regrets.

13. City

Amidst the fog
Beyond the silver linings,
Standing with her head held high
This city with her eternal shining.
The crowd travels beyond the roads
Bylanes spit a story of its own,
Few bonds break and build
Every soul has lessons to breathe.
Days are gone
Those memories remained,
Is it easy to travel those roads?
The city asked with a pale tone.
Rejected the signs
Accepted her own fate,
The city lies down silently...
Will I get another story to tell??

14. You

YOU

I met you at the strangest time
When things were scattering around,
You stayed till the last time
Gathering the scattered pieces.
Your eyes drooled me away
Your smile gave me a reason,
Your voice calmed me down
Your presence helped me sleep.
Sometimes it feels bitter
For everything I mess up,
Trust me I'm Very Sorry
Your Peace is all that Matters.
I will Stand by you like a shadow
Whenever and wherever you need,
Will stay awake and watch the Sunrise
I promise to be there for you Always…

15. Lonely…

Have you ever felt like there's no one but you left in this Dimension? Have you ever felt Lonely enough?
You think that being the way people want you to be will make them stay with you. You push yourself beyond the limits, just to seek that 5min presence. But all you get is just a reminder call that there was no one and there will be no one.
When it's a festive eve and you see your friends or family members or neighbours slowly leaving the house and mixing with the crowds, do you keep that buried within yourself or let your rage settle in?
All you're doing is sitting in your room. Gazing at those streets through that room window. The Clock is ticking in the background slowly. Sounds of people celebrating festivities at full pace. You put on your earphones and play music at full volume to cancel those eerie noises and you dim your lights.
Yes you're lonely. But doesn't it mean you're independent and capable enough? Loneliness teaches you to be the best version of yourself amidst the chaos. Loneliness is painful but to push yourself beyond that extra mile, sometimes all you need is self-time.

16. Manifest

You're The One I look up to,
Because you give me a Reason to Go on.
Your Smile is soothing,
It pushes me to keep it.
Your Eyes are Mythical,
Like a brush stroke on a blank canvas.
Your Soul is the purest,
Because you make people smile.
Your Calmness is everlasting,
It hushes all the noises.
Your voice is Healing potion,
Relieves all the stress and agonies.
Your anger kind of scares me,
But a lesson stays in.
Your Presence is Nothing Less than Peace,
Because you calm all the storms Down.
You're the One I need,
And not just moulded to a definition...

17. Hope

Seeking for a last chance
Trying to be better,
Agonies are getting stronger
Hope is what matters.
Truth to be told
Promises to be full,
Seconds are getting darker
Hope is what matters.
Choosing to be sang-froid
Being one is your only armour,
Fill up that void
Hope is what matters.
Soulful life is an ambition
Seconds are longer than hours,
Peace is the only destination
Hope is what matters.
Time ticking with a faint chime
Steps making you ponder,
Just a leap left to take
Hope is what matters.

18. Words

Words are still echoing in my ear
Tears of solitude climbing down my cheeks,
Will those sounds ever shutdown?
Or will they travel till I lay down?
Does asking this make me wrong?
Maybe I was a bitter truth that was let gone.
I don't ask you for forgiveness
I am still asking myself of my wrong doings
If I find any in this long journey,
I will repent on the epiphany.
You took out that kindness
Made it numb,
Does it still beat?
Asked the Soulless Being.
You travel now at ease
Making memories with your own,
Nothing but a simple question…
Do you still hold those Memories on?

19. Searching

25 storeys high
Looking at the sky,
Laying on the terrace
Searching for another try.
Regrets running over
Engulfed by the past,
Sunken in that Deep Sea
Searching for another trust.
Stepped on the wrong ground
There is nothing but an empty glance,
Too weak to stand again
Searching for another chance.
Fighting with Agony
Anxieties sticks with the Chime,
Ticking with that Irony
Searching for another Time.

20. Realisation...

You stand at the Horizon
In front of you lies a white wall,
You're finally in the seclusion
Look back… you've lost all.
Tranquillity comes at what cost?
Asked by the faint beating heart,
Nothing but emptiness
Answered by your lost soul.
The messy mind hushed
Do you miss the abyss…
Or the noxious side of it?
The beating heart paused for a bit
Maybe the memories were triggering…
Took a deep breath.
It wasn't the memories, but the habits calling.
Chaotic mind finally spoke
Your peace doesn't petrify your soul,
You should embrace that feeling
Self-realisation is all that beholds.

21. Life

LIFE… Simple to understand, Harder to achieve. Every one of us thinks this word needs to hold a deeper meaning. In search of that we lose those basic but innocent traits of Life. Sometimes it holds a meaning of Thousand Butterflies.

It can be a Person. An excuse. A wish. A need. Anything. Our Life is like a Lost Soul in a Desert. Even when he has clenched his thirst from the Oasis the Mirage doesn't stop. Yes, Life is made up of bits and bytes. It can be filled up till the brim with small moments and memories.

But what if that same Life turns to be a Bed of Thousand Thorns?

Yes, Small things do make our Life but what about the Void of those Big Pieces. Life is like a random puzzle of different Shapes and Sizes. Sometimes Big pieces are a Necessity. Just like our staple food. When that humungous piece goes missing, we feel claustrophobic and our very next thought is that LIFE is incompatible and incomplete. Really?

What about the remaining small pieces? It can fill up 70% of your pit. But rest of it solely depends upon you. If you wait for those Big Pieces, eventually that pit will turn into an Abyss. But… If you look on the bright side and see your Life as almost filled, maybe those voids will eventually nullify. Slowly and

steadily, one learns to make their own Breakfast.
Why do we forget those tiny little moments? Will it help you, if, after a decade, with a glass of wine you start regretting?

22. Hold My Hands

Hold My Hands…
And I will take you to the Brighter Side you never imagined.
Hold My Hands…
And I will tell you the Secrets why Constellation and Sky are a Perfect Match.
Hold My Hands…
And I will guide you through the Journey of a Lifetime.
Hold My Hands…
And I will prove to you that Silence speaks louder than Words.
Hold My Hands…
And I will make you Cherish each Second of your Life.
Hold My Hands…
And I will guide you from Dusk to Dawn.
Hold My Hands…
And I will Show you Not Everyone Leaves…

23. Lost Warrior

Landing on your face
Oppressed by the Society,
New Destinations still Vague
Expectations perished from Almighty.
Life is a bitter truth
Irritated of the closed ones
Nurturing the false hope
Eternal Peace can't be won.
Surprised of the backstabs?
Seeing it from times unknown
Inner regrets are up for grabs
Surveying the sky from Dusk till Dawn.
Northern Star guides your path
Ego's getting crushed to dust,
Validations are fake concerns
Empty bottle of pure Trust.
Rigorous revision of ultimate plans?
Extemporaneous goals you grabbed,
Numb heart is all that beats
Devastated by their words that stabbed.
Immaturity disappeared from the face
Negligence is your fighting key,

Glance of Loneliness is all you trace.
Loneliness is not an option
But a long-lost trail,
Stays with you Silently
Breaks itself when words fail.
Melody was your stand
You chose to avoid,
With a fixated zone to vent
Nothing left, but void.
Words started imprinting on page
Emotions flew through the ink,
Lines never left your side
Rhymes let the Feeling sink.

24. Mistake

Scrambled up by the memories
Was it so easy to forget?
Every moment we painted
You closed it in a wooden casket.
Everything was so bitter
You never took a second thought,
Maybe you were…
Just proving to be a broken Hope.
Stood there at your doorstep
When everything around you had faded,
And I stood there beside you
When you left and neglected.
Just wanted to be a fragment
And all the sorrows to take,
Got some strings attached…
Was it my Mistake?

25. Casa

Beyond those dark less travelled road
Lies a House at top of a Hill,
Silent, yet a story of its own
Murmurs within deep Inside.
No one to attend, no one to check
Dust of Time lies on the floor,
Broken mirrors with tint glass
Sunder's the Room from warm light.
Screaming in search of a Soul
Slowly loses the voice of its own,
Takes it as a Choice of Destiny
Goes on with those Daily Epiphanies.
Years passed by longing on those Memories
Which Faded away without any trace,
Looked up to the sky with a Smile
Conceive, that the Roof is Lost.
Yawned upon the fact of return
A Glory that is Long Lost,
It's just a rugged wooden work
Will it provide with a Stable Tale?
Ask yourself about the House you build
Fill it with the Vibes you thirst,

Base should be stronger than a Promise
And… The Print should be within your Fist…

26. Smile

Standing again on the edge
Neglected by the close ones,
Understood by none
Smile… It will pass.
Shouting at the top
Expecting ears to discern,
Heard only by The Room
Smile… It will pass.
Shedding down those tears
For whom ask those curious eyes,
Neglecting it since the time unknown
Smile… It will pass.
Smiling is the only solution?
Ask those tired lullabies,
Put on that mask again…
Smile… It will pass.

27. The Old Me

Hey little kid…
May I come in?
I see question in your eyes
Hold on, let me sit.
You really do have a soulful smile
I wonder those all were true,
You might be thinking
Who I am,
14 years journey was incredible champ.
I am you,
I am the one who misses you,
I am the one who trusts you,
I am the one who loves you.
Not because of those glittery eyes
Or rather for that mischievous smile.
I miss you,
Because of your soulful babble.
Open your ears
Pay some close attention,
These words are your war cry
The long journey ahead of you
Will feel like a Loop ride,

Buckle up yourself
Or else you will be cast aside.
You will think of giving it all up
Ending things on a harsh note,
Count yourself backwards
Not only the numbers but the words.
The hands beside will slowly fade
This will make you question yourself
Neither you nor they were wrong,
What was wrong, was the damn time…
You got your fair share of fun,
Or should I say a little over the brim,
Calm yourself and think straight
You needed a hand to stay
Then will come a dark phase
Every step will crumble in front of you
Try to look on the brighter side
Those steps break to give few stones to step.
It's time for me to go,
Etch these words within you,
Might help you on those gloomy days
You too standing on the green grass
Stay calm, and it will pass.

28. Nothing Is Easy

Look at his eyes
You will see the pain he felt,
Look at his shows
You will find the roads he went.
Look at his watch
You will see the time he wept,
Look at his hair
You will see the mess he dealt.
Look at his dress
You will see the sacrifices,
Look at his hands
You will see the stand-alone eagerness.
He stood there all alone
Waiting for that perfect time,
While everything was gone
Only thing that stayed was a clock's chime.

29. Will You...

Words are echoing down your spine
Those eyes are searching for the homely charm,
Spiralling down through the endless pit.
Will you grab a hand or a stick?

Mundane life is all that remains
Taunting you for the rest of your days,
Giving up is your only chance.
Will you hustle all the way or let your Life steer?

Your soul yearns for the olden days
Your heart skips a beat or two,
Two drops of emotion scatters down the cheeks.
Will you let it flow or conceal it with that smile?

Autumn is waiting around the corner
With pleasant mornings and cozy evenings.
Sitting on the bench all alone
Will you call it freedom or loneliness?

Your hands search for a stable time
The clock ticks with its endless chime,

Days are gone in the blink of an eye.
Will you halt for a while or go on with the ticking time?

30. Dead Deep Down

Sitting in a graveyard
Thinking about life,
My future's in the front yard
But there's no remaining time.
My past was kind of ruthless
Fighting till I'm breathless,
Suggestions are endless
Please Don't make a mess.
Regrets deep down
Anxiety is my friend
Hopes are going down
Is it the "DEAD END?"
Deserted by people
Promises were lies,
Searching for the one
But the time flies.
Standing on the edge
Mountain's pretty tall
Just checking the ledge
I forgive you all.

www.ingramcontent.com/pod-product-compliance
Lightning Source LLC
LaVergne TN
LVHW041252150826
845673LV00008B/2564

* 9 7 9 8 8 9 2 7 7 1 3 0 6 *